W9-DFF-415

SUGAR GROVE PUBLIC LIBRARY DISTRICT
54 Snow Street/P.O. Box 1049
Sugar Grove, IL 60554
(630) 466-4686

9/21/04

SUGAR GROVE PUBLIC LIBRARY DISTRICT
54 Snow St. / 466-4686
Hours: Mon. - Thurs. 10 am - 9 pm
Hours: Fri. & Sat. 10 am - 5 pm

War and Conflict in the Middle East™

The Suez Crisis

James W. Fiscus

The Rosen Publishing Group, Inc., New York

Published in 2004 by The Rosen Publishing Group, Inc.
29 East 21st Street, New York, NY 10010

First Edition

Library of Congress Cataloging-in-Publication Data

Fiscus, James W.
The Suez crisis / by James W. Fiscus.
    p. cm. — (War and conflict in the Middle East)
Summary: Examines the history behind Egypt's push for control of the Suez Canal and the battle waged against Britain, France, and Israel, plus biographical notes on leaders and a look at the effects of the crisis.
Includes bibliographical references and index.
ISBN 0-8239-4550-2 (library binding)
1. Sinai Campaign, 1956—Causes—Juvenile literature. 2. Egypt—History—Intervention, 1956—Juvenile literature. 3. Israel—Foreign relations—France—Juvenile literature. 4. France—Foreign relations—Israel—Juvenile literature. 5. Israel—Foreign relations—Great Britain—Juvenile literature. 6. Great Britain—Foreign relations—Israel—Juvenile literature. 7. Suez Canal (Egypt)—Juvenile literature. [1. Sinai Campaign, 1956—Causes. 2. Egypt—History—Intervention, 1956. 3. Israel—Foreign relations—France. 4. France—Foreign relations—Israel. 5. Israel—Foreign relations—Great Britain. 6. Great Britain—Foreign relations—Israel. 7. Suez Canal (Egypt)] I. Title. II. Series.
DS110.5.F57 2003
956.04'4—dc21

2003009383

CONTENTS

During the 1956 Suez Crisis, three nations joined together to attack Egypt. Each acted for its own reasons. Great Britain and France wanted to take control of the Suez Canal to "protect" it from Egypt. They also wanted to bring down the Egyptian government of Gamal Abdel Nasser. Israel fought the war as part of its continuing struggle with its Arab neighbors. It had become independent only eight years earlier. The failure of the three allies to achieve their goals in the face of international pressure marks the retreat of the old colonial nations from the Middle East. The retreat of the two European powers allowed the entry of the United States and the Soviet Union into the area.

To understand the Suez Crisis, one should start with a fast look at a map of the region (map 1, page 6). The yellow lines on the oceans show the sea-lanes used by ships carrying cargo from Europe or North America through the Suez Canal to India and Asia. Before the canal was built,

ships had to sail around Africa (the red lines). The canal cut about 4,500 miles (7,242 kilometers) off the voyage from England to India. Even for today's modern ships, the canal makes a big difference. A cargo ship going from London to Bombay (recently renamed Mumbai), India, takes about seventeen days if the ship goes through the Suez Canal. Sailing around Africa increases the trip to about twenty-nine days.

The canal remains important. Most of the world's cargo still moves across the oceans. More than 14 percent of all cargo and more than a quarter of the world's oil are shipped through the Suez Canal.

As you read, remember that war is always ugly. In war, people have their arms and legs shattered by explosions. In war, people die in pain. Even in this small war in Suez, more than 2,000 soldiers died while another 6,000 were wounded. We need to understand why nations go to war and that there is no glory in war.

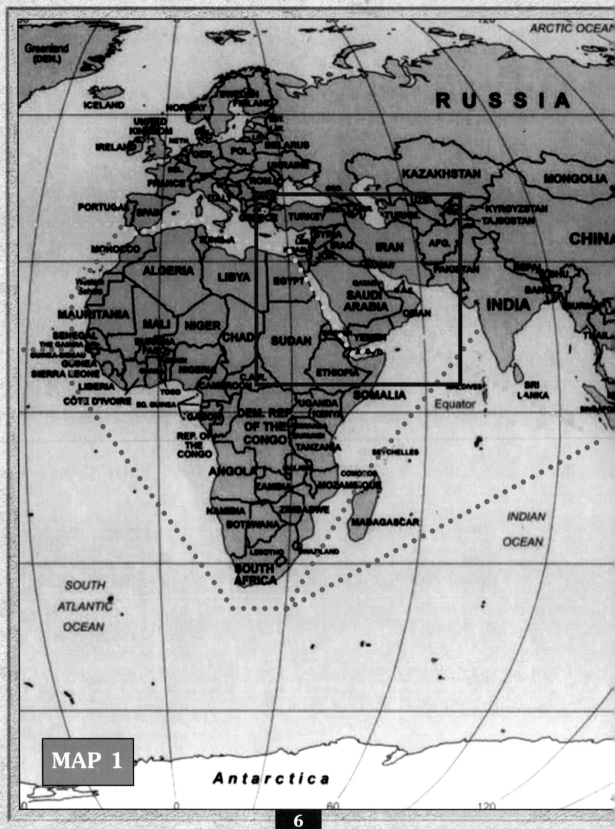

MAP 1

Antarctica

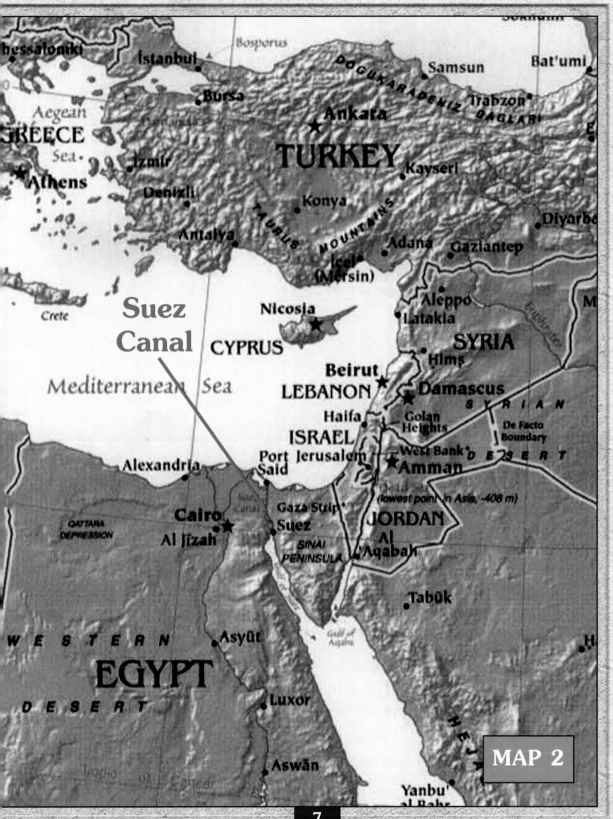

Suez
Canal

MAP 2

CHAPTER 1

BACKGROUND FOR WAR: WHY SUEZ?

L ook at the map of the Middle East (map 2, page 7). The Isthmus of Suez is a strip of land about 100 miles (161 km) wide. It divides the Mediterranean Sea from the Red Sea and the Indian Ocean. The Suez Canal crosses the isthmus. It allows ships to move freely between the oceans of the world. At the same time, the isthmus marks the division between Asia and Africa. The isthmus is also a bridge. Invaders crossed the isthmus to attack Egypt while Egyptian armies crossed it to attack their enemies to the east.

A Canal Across Suez

The first canal between the Nile River and the Red Sea was dug through the sands nearly 4,000 years ago when the pharaohs ruled Egypt. Over the following centuries, the canal filled with silt and was redug by Egyptians, Greeks, Romans, and Arabs. Interest in a canal stayed alive through the following centuries. Nothing happened, however, until the 1700s and 1800s when the European nations spread their trading and colonial empires across the world.

In 1854, Muhammad Said, the khedive (governor) of Egypt, gave a French company the right to build a canal across Suez. Muhammad Said gave the company a ninety-nine-year charter (lease) to run the canal. After stock was sold, Said owned just less

An ocean liner makes a stop along the Suez Canal in Egypt during the 1920s. By then, the canal had become a crucial link between the Mediterranean and Asia.

than half of the company. France owned most of the rest. The canal was finished a decade later in August 1869. Water from the Red Sea mixed with water from the Mediterranean.

The khedive had spent huge amounts of money building the canal. He had also spent money on many extravagant projects and on high living. Egypt's debt ballooned from 7 million British pounds to nearly 100 million pounds in thirteen years. The British seized the khedive's stock in 1879 to pay the interest on his debt. France remained the largest shareholder in the Suez Canal Company. Egypt was now out and Britain was in as the second largest shareholder.

Egyptian tax money had paid more than half the cost of the canal, and thousands of Egyptians had died building it. As the canal finally became a success, Egypt would see little benefit. In 1882, England landed troops at Alexandria and took over the country. Although Egypt officially became independent from Britain in 1936, the British consul general controlled Egypt until after World War II (1939–1945).

World War II weakened the ability of the European colonial nations to hold on to their colonies. The European nations had suffered major damage in the war and their economies were in trouble. The original people in the colonies were also less willing to live under foreign rulers. Anticolonial rebellions swept through Asia and Africa.

The Cold War and a Clash of Empires

At the end of World War II, the Soviet Union and its army occupied Eastern Europe. It also appeared ready to take over

Western Europe. The victory of the Communists in China three years later, in 1948, appeared to threaten Japan and the rest of east Asia. The United States and its allies saw the map of the world suddenly turning "red" (in other words, Communist) from Europe to Asia. The struggle between the eastern and western blocs, called the Cold War, had started.

The Founding of Israel

During the second century AD, Roman armies forced most of the Jewish population of ancient Judaea and Palestine into exile. Throughout their exile, Jews were attacked because they were not Christians. Anti-Semitism (hatred of Jews) exploded once again in Russia and eastern Europe during the nineteenth century, bringing widespread violence. In reaction to the violence, the Zionist movement was founded and began working to establish a safe homeland for Jews in Palestine. During World War II, the Nazis in Germany set up death camps that operated like factories to slaughter millions of people, mostly Jews. After Germany's defeat, many of the surviving Jews fled to Palestine.

In 1948, the Jews in Palestine announced the creation of the State of Israel. Israel's Arab neighbors saw the new nation as a form of European colonialism. They also rejected one of the basic ideas of Zionism, that Jews had a right to return to their former homeland. The Arabs attacked in May 1948. Eight months later, it was over, and Israel had survived as a nation.

Some 700,000 Palestinians had become refugees during the war. Israel, however, was not prepared to let refugees return to their homes. Likewise, Arab states were not willing to take them in and make them citizens. Fighters from the refugee camps crossed the border to attack Israel. The Palestinian and Egyptian irregulars (troops that were not part of Egypt's regular army) attacking Israel were called fedayeen.

The fedayeen raided Israel. The Israeli Defense Force (IDF) defended the country. The fedayeen then raided the West Bank, the Gaza Strip, and the Sinai Peninsula. Israeli historian Benny Morris (writing with British reporter Ian Black) says that wanting to stop the fedayeen raids was the major reason Israel attacked Egypt in 1956.

Prime Minister David Ben-Gurion signs documents that proclaim the existence of the State of Israel. Foreign Minister Moshe Shertok *(right)* looks on during the May 17, 1948, ceremony in Tel Aviv, the capital of the new nation.

The war was triggered, however, by a change in the military balance of power between Israel and Egypt. Following the 1948 war, Israel's military was far superior in both equipment and training to those of its neighbors. In 1955, Egypt obtained modern weapons from the Soviet Union. The weapons were delivered through Czechoslovakia. This deal became known as the Czech arms deal.

When they learned of the Czech arms deal, IDF chief of staff Moshe Dayan and other IDF generals asked the Israeli government for permission to attack Egypt before the new weapons reached the Arab country. The generals feared that the Egyptians would become too powerful for Israel to defeat.

Making the situation worse, in September 1955, Egypt closed the Straits of Tiran to Israeli shipping. The straits are at the Red Sea opening of the Gulf of Aqaba, which separates the east bank of the Sinai Peninsula from Arabia. Blocking the straits meant that the Israeli port of Elath at the head of the gulf was cut off from world trade. Egypt had closed the Suez Canal to Israeli shipping during the 1948 war. Closing the straits meant that Israeli ships had to sail around Africa to reach Asian ports.

Revolution in Egypt

The Turkish Ottoman Empire had ruled Egypt for 300 years. The empire was abolished after World War I (1914–1918) and Egypt became independent from Turkey. Despite Egyptian independence, Britain continued to control Egypt.

When the 1948 war erupted with Israel, Egypt was not ready. Egypt's ruler, King Farouk, had spent large amounts of money on palaces and personal pleasure. Little money went to supply his army. Many Egyptian soldiers went into battle with guns that could not fire. Farouk lost the loyalty of his army.

On January 25, 1952, British troops in the Suez Canal Zone fired on a crowd of Egyptians. More than forty Egyptians were killed. The next day, rioters in Cairo attacked both foreigners and the Egyptian government. Martial law (control of civil law enforcement and courts by the military) failed to stop the riots. In July, a coup d'état by the Egyptian army forced Farouk and his government from power. (A coup d'état is when a government is tossed out of power by force, usually by the military.)

While the riots triggered the coup, the underlying cause was the army's anger over the failure of the 1948 war. There was also discontent in the army over the need to break up the large estates owned by the Egyptian elites. Many officers saw the concentration of land ownership as a major cause of Egypt's economic problems.

The leader of the new Revolutionary Command Council (RCC) that ran the country was Lieutenant Colonel Gamal Abdel Nasser. Most of the nation wanted a rapid return to civilian government. The army officers, however, did not give up their control. Elections were delayed. Nasser pushed through a new constitution in 1956. It granted the president great power to run the nation. Nasser became president under the new constitution.

New Government, Old Problems

There were still problems after the coup. The new government still did not control the Suez Canal. More than 80,000

British troops remained on Egyptian soil. An agreement for the departure of the British was reached in 1953. Various details delayed the signing of the agreement. Finally, in July, the United States stepped in. President Dwight D. Eisenhower told Egypt that if it signed a canal agreement with Britain, the United States would give it economic aid. He also promised to help strengthen the Egyptian military. An agreement was signed between Britain and Egypt in late 1954. British troops would leave by June 1956. Britain and its allies kept the right to send troops back to the Suez Canal Zone should Turkey or any member of the Arab League be attacked.

The agreement eased problems with Egypt but increased tensions with Israel. The British troops along the canal were a shield between Egypt's main military forces and Israel. Israel's leaders feared that removal of the British would increase the chances of an attack by Egypt. (Nasser and other Arab leaders continued to call loudly for the destruction of Israel.)

Three weeks after the British-Egyptian agreement, President Eisenhower promised $40 million in economic and military aid to Egypt. America also agreed to consider helping build a dam at Aswan on the Nile River. The offer of aid for the Aswan High Dam would unintentionally help bring on the 1956 war.

With British troops leaving, Egypt would have to defend the canal with its own army. However, the 1948 war had shown the Egyptian army to be incompetent, and things had not changed since then.

Egypt needed modern weapons to protect its borders. Egypt also considered the truce that ended the fighting in 1948 a temporary delay in the battle to "liberate" Palestine from Israel. Perhaps most important, Nasser's power rested on the army. If he could not get modern weapons, the army would replace him with a leader who could do so.

The United States, Britain, and France had agreed in 1950 not to sell arms to any of the nations that had been involved in the 1948 war. While the ban included sales to both Israel and Egypt, the French continued to sell weapons to Israel. Egypt

An enthusiastic citizen embraces Egyptian prime minister Lieutenant Colonel Gamal Abdel Nasser above a throng of Egyptians on July 31, 1954. The seventy-two-year British occupation of the Suez Canal Zone had just ended, leaving Egypt in a new position of strength.

was out in the cold. (America did offer military aid but with conditions attached that Nasser felt he could not accept.)

Nasser turned to the Soviet Union. In exchange for Egyptian cotton, the Soviets sold modern arms to Egypt in 1955. The weapons were sent by way of Czechoslovakia in the Czech arms deal. Egypt would soon receive hundreds of jet aircraft, tanks, submarines, and other equipment.

Modernizing Egypt's Economy

On a map, Egypt looks to be a large country. But only 5 percent of Egypt's land can be farmed without massive irrigation projects. The Nile River Delta and a narrow strip of land along each side of the river have traditionally fed Egypt's people. Because the flow of the Nile varies throughout the year, it is not a dependable source of water for large irrigation projects. For the last 150 years, Egypt's population has grown rapidly. Farmland and economic development have not kept up.

Cliffs rising at Aswan 700 miles south of the Mediterranean make it the natural place at which to dam the Nile. A high dam at Aswan would give Egypt a steady flow of irrigation water for the entire year. Planners hoped to increase Egypt's farmland by 30 percent. A new dam would also provide electrical power for new industries. Nasser saw the Aswan High Dam as a way to move Egypt into the modern world. He also thought it would be a powerful symbol of Egypt's independence.

Egypt did not have enough money to complete the project. While the United States had said it might help, no money had yet been offered. The Czech arms deal forced America to

The site of the construction of the Aswan High Dam in Aswan, Egypt, circa May 9, 1964. More than 25,000 workers were employed in this ambitious project, which provided electrical power to Egypt and helped irrigate a great deal of land along the Nile River.

talk seriously with Egypt. America's promise was in part an effort to stop the Soviets from gaining more influence in the Middle East. America and Britain agreed to provide aid to help strengthen Egypt's economy. The aid would help Egypt to qualify for a loan from the World Bank. The loan would then be used to build the dam. With the promise of British and American aid to build the Aswan High Dam, Nasser appeared to have achieved his greatest goal. His victory seemed complete.

But Nasser knew little of the world outside of Egypt. He continued to give speeches that ranted against the conditions Britain, America, and the World Bank were attaching to the money for the dam. He also made several trade deals with Communist nations.

Nasser's actions led to Western doubts about the decision to help build the Aswan High Dam. Further, American supporters of Israel argued that nothing should be done to strengthen any of Israel's enemies. Finally, Egypt was (and still is) a major producer of cotton. Politicians from the American South feared that building the dam would allow Egyptians to grow even more cotton. That would make Egyptian cotton a stronger competitor with American cotton.

President Eisenhower and Secretary of State John Foster Dulles also wanted to weaken Nasser. They hoped to stop his push for Arab nationalism. (Arab nationalism is the idea that all Arab nations should join together and form a single state.) Eisenhower and Dulles hoped that canceling money for the Aswan High Dam would lead to Nasser's fall from power.

On July 19, 1956, the Egyptian ambassador returned to Washington, D.C., just a month after the last British troops left the Suez Canal Zone. He told the press that Egypt would accept American and British aid in building the Aswan High Dam. On the next day, he met with Dulles. Before the ambassador could say anything, Dulles told him that America was withdrawing its offer to pay for the dam.

The Slide into War

Nasser and the Egyptians were enraged by the canceling of the deal. They also felt insulted by the manner in which the news had been delivered. Nasser immediately nationalized

President Gamal Abdel Nasser of Egypt watches the Soviet premier Nikita Khrushchev on May 14, 1964, during a ceremony heralding the construction of the Aswan High Dam, which was partly financed by the Soviets. This alliance between an Arab state and Communists worried America and its allies.

the Suez Canal. Egypt took control of the canal from the Suez Canal Company and seized its property. Most of the owners were French and British. Both governments owned large amounts of the stock in the company. Nasser said that the $100 million per year profit from shipping fees would be used to build the Aswan High Dam.

Britain and France threatened to use force to take back control of the canal. The Arab states quickly supported Egypt. So did the Soviet Union and India. Likewise, the Soviets immediately offered to finance the dam. Workers across the oil fields of the Middle East promised to cut off the flow of oil if Western nations attacked Egypt. Nasser had successfully defied France and Britain. He had also hit back at the United States. He had become a hero.

British prime minister Anthony Eden saw Nasser's actions as a threat to Britain's trade and economy. Britain had still not recovered from World War II. The nation had entered the war as the world's leading creditor. Britain ended the war as the world's leading debtor. World War II had been one of Britain's greatest victories. But in the wake of victory, the glory of the British Empire was vanishing as colonies became independent.

Many Western leaders feared Egypt would be unable to run the canal. Thus, the longer that Egyptians successfully ran the canal without problems, the more time there was to find a peaceful way out of the crisis. The debate soon moved to the United Nations. In October, the British, French, and Egyptians agreed to a set of principles that would control the canal. It appeared to the world as if a solution had been reached. But it was too late. Britain, France, and Israel had long before decided to wage a war.

French Colonial Wars and the Suez Crisis

France had two main reasons for joining the British and Israelis in their attack on Egypt. France still owned the majority of shares in the Suez Canal Company. That meant that when Egypt took control of the canal, France lost a great deal of money.

A quartet of Egypt's military police stand guard over the headquarters of the Suez Canal Zone at Ismailia in this photo from February 1955. Control of the canal was a major boost to Egyptian prestige and economic well-being.

The second reason is more complex, but it is no less important. France suffered its first major colonial loss when it was driven out of Vietnam in 1954. In the same year, a revolt started in Algeria against French rule. France had conquered Algeria during the nineteenth century and claimed that it was a part of metropolitan France. (In other words, it was as much a part of France as Paris.) In 1951, Algerians opposed to French rule organized the Front de Libération Nationale (FLN), or National Liberation Front. In 1954, the FLN's armed revolution began. Before it ended, the Algerian war for independence drew nearly half of the entire French army into the fight. More than 10,000 French soldiers and 70,000 Algerian fighters died. Thousands of civilians on both sides died.

With the Algerian war just under way in 1956, France was desperate to cut off foreign support to the FLN. Nasser was giving political and economic support to the FLN. The French knew that Egypt was also sending guns to Algeria to help fight the French army. In 1956, the French captured a large arms shipment that was moving from Egypt to Algeria aboard a small ship, the *Athos*. The ship carried enough guns to arm some 3,000 FLN fighters. Learning of the arms on the *Athos* was the final push France needed. When Nasser took over the canal, French leaders decided that they would pull Nasser from power. Removing Nasser, they thought, would uphold French honor and stop Egyptian support for the Algerians.

CHAPTER 2

CONSPIRACY FOR WAR

One of British prime minister Anthony Eden's first reactions to the nationalization of the canal was to declare, "The Egyptian [Nasser] has his thumb on our windpipe."

Even after one of Eden's legal advisers told him, "He's doing nothing illegal in nationalizing the canal," the prime minister remained ready for action, saying he did not care if Nasser's action was legal or not. Eden planned on stopping Nasser. Eden ordered his military leaders to prepare for an attack on Egypt.

Eden stated his reasons for wanting to reclaim the canal in a message to President Eisenhower: "If we take a firm stand over this now, we shall have the support of all the maritime powers. If we do not, our influence and yours throughout the Middle East will . . . be finally destroyed . . . [w]e must be ready, in the last resort, to use force to bring Nasser to his senses."

Eden's strong personal reaction may also have been partly because he was ill. Three years earlier, Eden had been operated on to remove gallstones. The stones had blocked the duct (tube) leading from his gallbladder. The surgeon bungled the operation. Another operation was tried and failed. Finally, a third operation managed to clear the duct. However, Eden remained in pain

News reporters question British prime minister Anthony Eden and his foreign secretary John Selwyn-Lloyd at 10 Downing Street in London, England, during the Suez Crisis on August 18, 1956.

and now had an infection of the duct that could not be cured. He took antibiotics to keep it under control.

The illness robbed Eden of his strength. He took amphetamines to boost his energy. We now know that amphetamines can drastically change a person's moods and make it hard for him or her to deal with problems. In 1956, the side effects were not well understood.

The combination of illness, amphetamines, and the stress of the crisis meant that Eden was sleeping only about five hours a night. Eden's health grew worse. His moods swung wildly, and his temper flared often. We cannot know how much Eden's health affected his judgment and ability to manage the crisis. It is almost certain, though, that it did.

In addition, the crisis had become a personal duel between Eden and Nasser, not a dispute between nations. Nasser represented the end of the British Empire, and Eden hated him. Eden had been Britain's foreign minister during the 1930s. He viewed Nasser as a potential Adolf Hitler, comparing Nasser to Britain's most hated enemy. The danger of making mistakes always goes up when national disputes become personal fights between leaders.

The Plotters Meet

Immediately after the 1956 war, all three of the attackers insisted that they had not planned the attack together. There had been, they said, no conspiracy to attack Egypt. It took nearly a decade for the true story to come out.

Throughout the summer, Britain and France had prepared their soldiers and sailors for war. Israel also prepared for war. At first, Britain and France planned to attack Egypt by themselves, moving to knock Nasser from power and seize the canal.

About a week after the nationalization of the canal, the French defense minister met with the director-general of Israel's defense ministry, Shimon Peres. The French defense minister asked Peres how long it would take Israel to conquer the Sinai. The question told the Israelis that France might be interested in a joint attack on Egypt. On September 1, Israeli prime minister David Ben-Gurion and IDF chief of staff Moshe Dayan received another message from the French. The French government asked if Israel was interested in joining a British and French attack on Egypt.

Over the next few weeks, the details of the operation fell into place. The Europeans called this attack Operation Musketeer. Israel called the attack Operation Kadesh. The French prime minister, Guy Mollet, did not yet tell Anthony Eden that France and Israel were planning to attack Egypt. The French did not trust the British. They feared the British would back out of the conspiracy. By working with Israel, Mollet ensured that France would have its war with Egypt.

French and Israeli military officials met again to work out the details of their attack. Mollet wanted the attack to happen before the end of October. Fall weather in the Mediterranean can bring severe storms. Bad weather would make the operation more dangerous. Mollet also wanted to

French premier Guy Mollet *(left)* shakes hands with British prime minister Anthony Eden during a meeting in London on October 30, 1956. The meeting had been called to address the conflict over the Suez Canal.

strike just before the American presidential election in early November. The French believed that President Eisenhower would be preoccupied by his campaign for reelection and would not want to go against the wishes of Jewish voters in the United States by undercutting Israel.

On the last day of the meetings, the French chief of staff told Dayan that it would be best if Israel attacked first and alone. France would enter the war after it had started. Dayan did not like the idea. He didn't want Israel to look like the only aggressor.

During the first week in October, the French finally told Anthony Eden of their plan. Israel would attack Egypt and drive toward the canal. Britain and France would then act to "protect" the canal, demanding that both Israel and Egypt pull back. The planners expected Egypt to refuse. British and French troops would then invade. Eden was, according to a French general, "thrilled at the idea." Back in London, Eden's top advisers tried to talk him out of the war, but he was firm. Eden continued with the plot. He did not tell his full cabinet or leaders of his political party, the Conservatives.

British, French, and Israeli leaders met at Sérves in France on October 22. Israeli prime minister Ben-Gurion suggested a plan to carve up the region. Lebanon would be divided. Israel would seize the southern fifth of Lebanon, as far north as the Litani River. Syria—under a pro-Western government installed by force—would take the north. The center of Lebanon would become a Christian state. Jordan would also be divided. Israel would take the West Bank while

Iraq would take over the land east of the Jordan River (Iraq was still ruled by a pro-Western king who had been placed in power by the British). Israel would capture and hold Sharm el-Sheikh, the Egyptian base overlooking the Straits of Tiran. The French did not want that large a war and killed the idea immediately. (During the 1967 Arab-Israeli war, Israel took the West Bank and the Sinai. Later, in March 1978, following a Palestinian attack on a civilian bus, Israel took Lebanese territory to the Litani and supported the Christian South Lebanese Army.)

For his part, Ben-Gurion objected to the idea that Israel would attack first. But the British would not join the attack unless they could claim to be acting in defense of the canal. Israel finally agreed.

Putting the Plan in Writing

Representatives of all three nations signed an agreement to attack Egypt. Israel would begin its attack and then Britain and France would "appeal" to Egypt and Israel to stop fighting. The European nations agreed to start bombing Egypt within thirty-six hours of the start of the war. Israel agreed that it would not attack Jordan. (Britain had a defense agreement with Jordan.) At the same time, the French signed a separate agreement with Israel promising to station French fighter jets in Israel to protect the country against Egyptian air attacks. The war was set for October 29, 1956.

As the Suez Crisis built, President Eisenhower and Secretary of State Dulles kept trying to avoid a war in the

Middle East. Events in Eastern Europe, however, also called for their attention. Riots started in a number of countries occupied by the Soviets. The most serious riots were in Hungary. Hungarians attacked Soviet Red Army units. Reports said that members of the Hungarian army had gone over to the anti-Soviet rebels. Soviet troops first withdrew, then smashed back against the rebels on November 4. They had crushed the rebellion by the middle of the month. Eisenhower and Dulles had to divide their attention between the Hungarian rebellion and the Suez Crisis.

On Saturday, October 27 (two days before the planned attack), Eisenhower sent a message to Israel telling Ben-Gurion that America was concerned by Israel's call-up of its army reserves. Israeli intelligence had spread the rumor that Iraq had sent troops into Jordan to attack Israel. Eisenhower told Israel that there were no Iraqi troops in Jordan. The Israelis saw the message as confirming that America had been fooled and had no idea that war was about to start.

CHAPTER 3

THE WAR

As the war neared, Israeli spies scored several important intelligence victories.

- During 1956, Israel's intelligence services, Aman and Mossad, changed their targets from seeking information about the fedayeen to trying to find out what the Egyptian army was doing. (Aman was the intelligence branch of the IDF. Mossad was Israel's civilian secret intelligence service.) The operations were so successful that when the Suez War started, Israel knew where the Egyptian army was stationed in Gaza and the Sinai down to the level of army companies.

- As mentioned earlier, Israel fooled both the Americans and the Egyptians into thinking that their attack would be against Jordan and not the Sinai. Israel sent reserve troops to the Jordanian border, telling them that Jordan was the target. Israel's deception was one of the reasons Egypt moved troops out of the Sinai.

- Finally, hours before Israel attacked, information from spies told an IDF fighter jet where to fly to shoot down an Egyptian transport plane over the Mediterranean. The shooting killed many important commanders as the transport carried eighteen members of the Egyptian general staff. (The general staff of an army is in overall

Egyptian soldiers emerge from trenches during practice maneuvers near the Gaza Strip before the Suez Crisis. They are armed with Czechoslovakian-made machine guns.

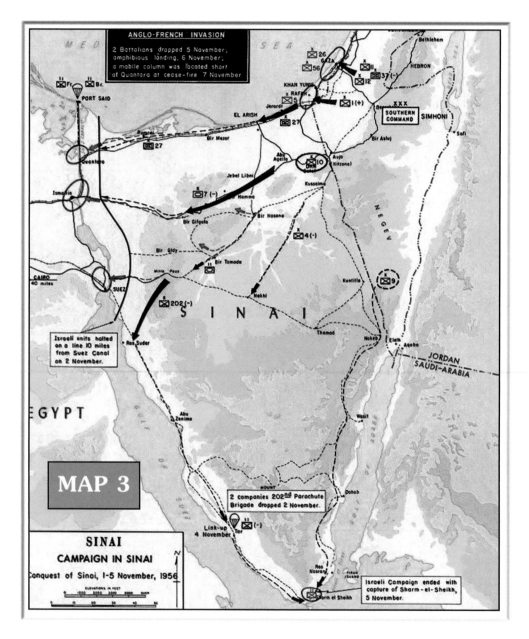

ANGLO-FRENCH INVASION
2 Battalions dropped 5 November;
amphibious landing, 6 November;
a mobile column was located short
of Quantara at cease-fire 7 November.

Israeli units halted
on a line 10 miles
from Suez Canal
on 2 November.

MAP 3

2 companies 202ⁿᵈ Parachute
Brigade dropped 2 November.

Link-up
4 November

Israeli Campaign ended with
capture of Sharm-el-Sheikh,
5 November.

SINAI
CAMPAIGN IN SINAI
Conquest of Sinai, 1-5 November, 1956

Israel attacked swiftly through the Sinai Peninsula on October 29, 1956. Its army and air force controlled the three main routes across the desert. Israeli forces stopped ten miles short of the Suez Canal.

command of troops and military planning.) The mission was not reported publicly until more than thirty years had passed. The blow to Egypt's commanders was so great that Dayan told the pilot when he landed, "Let's go drink to the second half [of the war]."

Geography of the Sinai

The Sinai Peninsula is a triangle, with its base in the north along the Mediterranean Sea and its point jabbing south. (Take a look at map 3, page 34). The Gulf of Suez and the Gulf of Aqaba flank the southern part of the peninsula. The Straits of Tiran separate the Sinai from Arabia. Most of the peninsula is rocky desert, cut by old streambeds that left deep gullies, called wadis. The southern part of the Sinai is covered with high hills and low mountains.

To the north, three main routes cross the peninsula. The northern route hugs the coast from Gaza to the canal. The central route runs west from Israel through the Bir Gifgafa Pass and on to the canal at Ismailia. The southern route runs west from Israel through the Mitla Pass to the southern end of the canal. All three routes were defended by the Egyptian army. To threaten the canal as planned, Israel had to drive the Egyptians from the peninsula.

The Egyptian Army

Egypt had prepared strong fortifications near the Israeli border. They had been designed and built with the help of German military advisers. All used bunkers, sandbags, mines, and concertina wire (barbed wire formed into long coils) for protection. The main strong points were around Rafah in Gaza, El Arish near the coast in the Sinai, and Abu Ageila farther south. All of the major roads, road junctions, and communication centers were guarded by prepared defenses.

Egypt's army contained 90,000 troops. Normally, 60,000 of them were in the Sinai facing Israel. But as Britain and France moved forces to the Mediterranean in clear preparation for an attack on Egypt, half of the Sinai garrison was moved to the Suez Canal Zone or to the Nile River Delta to defend Alexandria and Cairo. Only 30,000 remained in the Sinai.

The Egyptian movement of troops was not a bad plan. Nasser and his generals believed that Britain and France would attack at Alexandria and at the Suez Canal Zone to bring down his government. The belief was reasonable. The rumors of a war with Jordan spread by Israeli intelligence also encouraged Egypt to see the greatest danger in the west.

At the start of the war, Egypt had two infantry divisions supported by about 200 tanks and self-propelled guns (artillery) facing Israel. Major General Ali Amer headed the Eastern Command.

The Israeli Army

Throughout the war, Israel had to keep strong forces on its borders with Jordan, Lebanon, and Syria to guard against attack. The Israeli army was better trained and better led than Egypt's.

Israel prepared 45,000 troops to attack Egypt. The main attacking force was the Southern Command under Colonel Asaf Simhoni. It consisted of six infantry brigades, three armored (tank) brigades, and one airborne (parachute) brigade. Six other brigades formed a reserve (emergency) force in the center and the north. The force had between 200 and 250 tanks.

The British and French Armies

The British and French used the islands of Cyprus and Malta as the main bases for their attack. British forces included an infantry division, an airborne brigade, and a Royal Marine commando brigade. The French supplied an airborne division, a parachute battalion, and a light mechanized brigade. Both sent their navies into action, including six aircraft carriers, cruisers, destroyers, and other ships. The carriers and various military airfields sent hundreds of modern fighters and bombers into action.

The War in the Sinai

Israel planned to send three brigades against the Egyptian fortifications at Abu Ageila and Um Katef. After taking those positions, the force would strike through the center of the Sinai and capture the pass at Bir Gifgafa. A secondary attack called for one battalion of the parachute brigade (paratroopers) to jump into the Mitla Pass. The paratroopers were to take the pass and hold it until the rest of the brigade reached them by road. The parachute brigade was led by Ariel Sharon, who became prime minister decades later.

Later in the attack, three brigades would take Rafah. This move would cut Gaza off from the Sinai. Part of this force would then drive west along the coast toward the canal. Another brigade would follow the southern shore of the Sinai to take Sharm el-Sheikh at the tip of the peninsula. All Israeli forces would stop ten miles (sixteen kilometers) from the canal.

Members of the Israeli military inspect Egyptian tanks captured during the conflict. Israel captured key positions on the Sinai Peninsula very early in the war.

War began with the paratroopers dropping from their planes at the eastern end of the Mitla Pass on the night of October 29. The rest of the brigade arrived early the next morning. The Egyptian commander in the area realized that the attack was not just another raid. He ordered two brigades that were west of the canal to cross over and reinforce the troops holding the pass. They reached the Mitla Pass in time to strengthen its defense. (The Egyptian 1st Armored Division was also ordered to cross the canal to reinforce the area around the Gifgafa Pass.)

Sharon's troops tried for several days to drive the Egyptians from the Mitla Pass and failed. The Egyptians fought hard in hand-to-hand combat. They struggled to hold the ledges and caves that lined the pass. Eventually, Sharon's parachute troops seized the mouth of the Mitla Pass. The Egyptians still held most of the pass, blocking the Israeli advance in the south.

In the center, the 4th Infantry Brigade swept through the Egyptians at Kusseima on October 29. Many of the Egyptians fled without a fight. The Israeli brigade divided. Part of the brigade moved into the center of the Sinai to protect the paratroopers' northern flank. The remainder of the force swung north to attack the fortifications around Abu Ageila.

On the next night, an Israeli infantry brigade attacked the Um Katef fortifications that defended the east side of Abu Ageila. The Israeli attack was clumsy, with troops attacking as they arrived rather than waiting and attacking together. The Israelis charged straight at the front of the Egyptian positions rather than moving around the flanks (sides), which they could have done. The Egyptians easily drove them off.

The Israelis attacked for two days. Units sent forward in disorganized attacks were defeated easily. Kenneth Pollack, in his book *Arabs at War*, calls the Israeli attacks at Abu Ageila "inept." The Egyptians fought effectively on the defense and stopped the Israeli advance.

While the main force attacked the front of the Egyptian lines, a small unit under Lieutenant Colonel Avraham Adan swung around the Egyptian flank. Adan's unit was made up of one company of infantry in half-tracks (lightly armored trucks with tank treads in back and wheels in the front), one company of infantry in trucks, and one company of World War II–era Sherman tanks (map 4, page 41).

Once at the rear of the Egyptians at Um Katef, Adan captured the important crossroads at the village of Abu Ageila. He then attacked the Egyptians holding the Rafah Dam, which protected Um Katef. The Egyptians counterattacked. Fortunately for Adan's men, the Egyptian attacks were weak and poorly led. The troops moved forward and fired their guns for some minutes, trying to destroy the Israelis by fire alone. They made no effort to either maneuver around Adan's troops or to attack directly with their greater numbers.

While this fighting was going on, Egyptian reinforcements were on the way. Two tank companies and a battalion of infantry had been sent by the Egyptian command to support the defenders of Abu Ageila. This force stumbled into the rear guard of Adan's troops at the crossroads.

Adan broke off from the main Egyptian positions to fight the new threat.

The Egyptians again tried to attack with firepower alone. They refused to send troops to attack the small force facing them. Adan swung troops around to the Egyptian flank and the Egyptians fled. Adan turned back and finally captured the Rafah Dam defenses. The main Egyptian position, however, held firm. It was taken only after Nasser ordered a retreat from the Sinai on November 1.

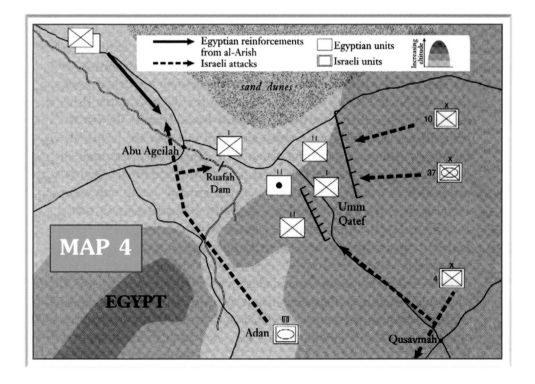

Lieutenant Colonel Adan's attack on the Egyptians at the Rafah Dam and Abu Ageila defended the rear of Um Katef. The dotted lines show Israel's disorganized frontal attacks on Um Katef.

As the fighting continued at Abu Ageila, the Israeli 7th Armored Brigade circled around the town and drove west toward the canal. The Egyptians sent an armored division toward the Israelis, but the unit was slowed by heavy attacks from the Israeli air force. The Israelis also slowed their advance, fearing that Britain and France would not keep their words and attack.

On October 30, the British and French called for both sides to stop fighting and withdraw from the canal. They also demanded the right to take control of the canal zone. The next day, British and French planes struck. In spite of the war, the Egyptians did not have planes flying protective combat air patrols above their bases. The British and French destroyed more than 150 Egyptian planes on the ground.

The bombing of bases across Egypt did not fully accomplish what the British and French had expected. They had thought the bombing would terrify the Egyptian people and cause them to throw Nasser out. Bombing alone, however, has never broken the will of a nation. The massive bombing of Britain, Germany, and Japan during World War II destroyed entire cities. It did not break the will of the people living in the cities. It is odd, then, that the British thought they would break the Egyptian people with air power. Nasser's reaction to the bombing was to have the army give guns to the people so they could help defend the nation.

Nasser realized that the British and French would soon invade the Suez Canal Zone. He did not want a large part of his army cut off and ordered Egyptian forces in the Sinai to

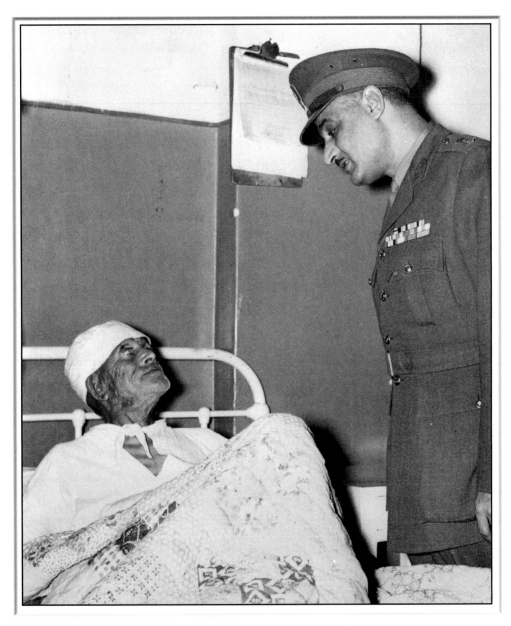

President Nasser visits a refugee in a hospital in Gaza, one of the casualties of an Israeli attack that took place on April 5, 1956. Gaza would be annexed by Israel during the Six-Day War in 1967. Israel wanted it as a buffer zone against further attacks from Egypt.

withdraw west of the canal. The order reached the troops on November 1. The Egyptian armored division immediately turned around and recrossed the canal. Israeli troops then advanced without a fight.

At the base of the Gaza Strip, Israel struck Rafah the same day. While some Egyptian troops fought bravely, many more fled. With the fall of Rafah, Gaza was cut off and soon fell to Israeli troops. Pollack reports that the Egyptians failed to counterattack or coordinate their attacks at Rafah. After taking Rafah, part of the Israeli forces headed west to join the attack on Abu Ageila. Now, however, the Israelis waited for the Egyptians to withdraw, which they did. By midnight on the night of November 2, nearly all Egyptian forces in the Sinai had started to retreat. The Israeli army stopped ten miles short of the canal, as planned.

By the end of the day, the Egyptians had either been surrounded or crossed the canal. An Israeli infantry brigade was slogging down the Aqaba coast toward Sharm el-Sheikh while some of Sharon's paratroopers attacked down the Gulf of Suez coast.

On November 3, the United Nations General Assembly demanded an immediate cease-fire. Both the Soviet Union and the United States voted for the resolution. Israel at first accepted the cease-fire, then imposed conditions that made it impossible for Egypt to accept. An early cease-fire would have destroyed the British and French excuse for their attacks and Sharm el-Sheikh had not yet fallen. (Sharm el-Sheikh finally surrendered on November 5 and Israel's war was over.)

British forces move through the city of Port Said, Egypt, during the French-British invasion, as an oil installation burns in the background, on November 10, 1956. The British eventually took control of the city.

The Attack on Suez

The British and French commanders had originally planned to land at Alexandria and march to Cairo to remove Nasser from power. The Egyptians expected this move. However, the British government ordered a change in the plan. While destroying Nasser was the real reason for the attack, the public reason was to protect the canal. The British public would not accept the Alexandria landing. (Nasser undercut

A trio of Egyptians survey the rubble of Port Said on November 8, 1956. Parts of the city were destroyed during the British-French invasion. The battle for the port city was the last one of the war.

the public reason for the attack by sinking a number of ships in the canal and blocking the waterway.)

The plan was changed to an attack on Port Said (west of the canal) and Port Fuad (east of the canal) on the Mediterranean. Troops would then march down the long causeway that flanked the canal to take the Suez at the southern end.

The infantry attack started on November 5. After heavy air attacks, British paratroopers jumped near Port Said while French paratroopers dropped at Port Fuad. There was hard fighting, but by the end of the day, most of Port Said and all of Port Fuad were held by the allies. The paratroopers had also captured the bridges that led from the cities to the causeway flanking the canal.

The Egyptians tried to retake the bridge held by the French, but their attacks were, in Kenneth Pollack's words, "nothing more than mad charges, which the French beat back with ease." Early the next day, the British landed troops from their ships to strengthen their forces at Port Said. There was little resistance from the Egyptians. British and French forces were ordered to cease fire at midnight, and the war was over.

The Anglo-French force had cleared the way so that they could march south and seize the canal. Instead, they stopped the advance of their troops with Nasser still in power. Why did the three allies give up just as they seemed ready to totally defeat Egypt?

CHAPTER 4

IMPOSED PEACE AND IMPACT OF THE WAR

The fast answer as to why the British and French stopped is that while the Suez War of 1956 was short, it was long enough for the United States and the Soviets to force a peace. The Middle East had not been a big focus for American foreign policy. The Suez Crisis forced Eisenhower and Dulles to give the region their top attention.

Eisenhower had commanded the Allied armies that fought in western Europe during World War II. He understood war. He

was also outraged by armed aggression. The United States, Britain, and France had signed a tripartite (three-party) agreement in 1950. The agreement pledged the three nations to not sell arms to any Middle East nation. It also said that if any state in the Middle East were attacked, the three powers would act to protect the victim of the attack. Eisenhower believed the United States was bound by its word to uphold that promise.

In March 1956, Eisenhower told Secretary Dulles, "In a general conflict [in the Middle East] the United States would follow its traditional policy of supporting the aggrieved [attacked] side and oppose aggression." Dulles agreed.

After the Israeli attack, Eisenhower told his advisers that the war was not acceptable. When warned that action against Israel

British soldiers look through captured Egyptian weapons after the end of hostilities in November 1956. Though Egypt lost the war militarily, the victors ultimately gained little.

British troops check out a Russian tank that had been delivered to Port Said to help the Egyptians. Other captured items included a new type of rocket launcher and two thirty-ton Russian cannons.

could cost him the election, the president said, "I don't care in the slightest whether I'm reelected or not. I feel we must make good on our word." Later the same day, he told the highest British diplomat in Washington that Britain and America must keep their word and stop aggression.

Underlying Eisenhower's anger was his belief that many Arab states were uneasy about Nasser's actions and were moving closer to the West in reaction. The Israeli attack stopped that movement cold. Eisenhower felt the situation could still be saved if America, Britain, and France kept their word to oppose aggression. The British and French attack on Egypt destroyed that thin hope.

The Soviet reaction to the war was even stronger. After the British and French attacked, the Soviets promised to help Egypt. There was also a rumor that the Soviets had offered Egypt a quarter of a million "volunteers." (The volunteers would have been members of the Soviet army.) While the Soviets had not actually made the offer to send volunteers, the possibility of Soviet troops in Egypt made the situation far more dangerous. With both American and Soviet forces in the Middle East, a clash between the superpowers would be possible. Such a clash could lead to World War III. Eisenhower placed America's military on alert.

Anthony Eden's support at home was vanishing. His Conservative Party faced strong opposition from the Labor Party in Parliament. Opposition from the British public also grew. Several leading members of Eden's government had resigned to protest the war. Leading papers said the war was illegal and must stop.

Britain had been desperately short of money before the fighting started. With the war on, other nations had sold off their British pounds. Britain had to sell gold reserves to keep the pound from losing value. The reserves had fallen by 100 million pounds in a week. Britain desperately needed money, and only the United States could help.

America offered Britain a loan of $1.5 billion, but only if Eden accepted a cease-fire and agreed to leave Egypt. Anthony Eden had no choice. He accepted the money and the fact that he had lost his gamble to overthrow Nasser.

Likewise, France had its own political and economic problems. Some of its army was tied down in Algeria. Its economy was also weak. France had no choice but to go along with the British decision.

Israeli prime minister Ben-Gurion, however, was elated. Gaza and the Sinai were no longer Egyptian, he announced. He planned to hold on to the new territory. Eventually, though, Israel gave in to American economic and political pressure and agreed to withdraw. A United Nations Emergency Force (UNEF) entered the area. At first, it divided the parties at the cease-fire line in the Sinai. After Israel's withdrawal, the UNEF patrolled the border between Israel and Egypt. The UNEF remained on duty helping to keep the peace until just before the 1967 Arab-Israeli war.

British and French forces were out of Egypt by the end of December. Israel had withdrawn from most of the Sinai by the end of January 1957. Israel left Gaza and the Gulf of Aqaba in May.

Impact of the Crisis

The Suez Crisis was a turning point in history. The failure of Britain and France to impose their will on Egypt marked the end of old-style colonial control of the Middle East. Following Suez, many people in the Middle East and the rest of the world saw the Soviets as their defenders against Western domination. Pro-Western governments in Iraq and Libya soon fell to Arab nationalist regimes that followed Nasser's lead.

British prime minister Harold Macmillan *(left)*, Anthony Eden's successor, meets with Nasser *(second from left)* at the United Nations in New York City in September 1960. It was the first meeting between the two nations since the Suez Crisis.

Britain and France had expected to bring Nasser down. Instead, he rose to even greater power and influence. Both the British and French governments soon fell when they lost elections.

Before Suez, the United States had been interested in the Middle East, but it had not been deeply involved. After the Suez Crisis, America was sucked into the Middle East more and more. In January 1957, Eisenhower issued the Eisenhower Doctrine. This doctrine said that America would

The events of the Suez Crisis and subsequent wars against Arab states have made Israel a target for terrorism. Here, a suicide bomber has blown up a bus in downtown Jerusalem, killing sixteen people. Israeli retaliation soon followed in the form of attacks against the terrorist group Hamas, which has bases in the Israeli-occupied Gaza Strip.

use its military to defend any Middle Eastern nation attacked by the Communists.

Israel appeared the winner at Suez, even after withdrawing from Egyptian territory. However, the war marked a sharp turn by Israel toward the use of its military. Israeli power would be used again to gain territory in the 1967 war. The long war fought against the Palestinians in the West Bank and Gaza still continues, as does the Arab hatred of Israel. The war between Israelis and Palestinians seems as far from a peaceful solution now as it did in 1956.

In a final irony, the Aswan High Dam has been an ecological disaster. It has provided much-needed electrical power for industry and Egypt's cities. But stopping the Nile's natural flood cycle has injured both Egypt and the entire Mediterranean Sea. The annual flood of the Nile no longer sweeps stagnant water out of the Nile Delta. Deadly parasites have grown out of control. Thousands of people have been affected each year. For thousands of years, the rich silt left after the floods fertilized Egypt's land. Trapped behind the Aswan High Dam, the silt no longer enriches the farms of Egypt. The country has had to buy expensive chemical fertilizers instead. Worse yet, without the flood, intensive irrigation has led to a massive increase in the amount of salt in the soil. The salt kills crops. Finally, the rich organic silts from the jungles of central Africa no longer reach the Mediterranean. Shrimp and other sea life have been cut off from their natural food supply.

In the end, none of the parties in the war won.

Arab League An association of independent countries whose peoples mainly speak Arabic. It was founded in Cairo, Egypt, in 1946 to help end the British protectorates over Arab states in the area and to prevent the founding of a Jewish state in Palestine. The formal purpose of the league is to strengthen ties among the member states, coordinate their policies, and promote common interests. Also called the League of Arab States

Arab nationalism A political and cultural movement that began in the late nineteenth century. It grew in strength in the years between World Wars I and II. The core belief of Arab nationalism is that all Arab countries should be united as a single nation. The movement was largely led by secular (nonreligious) governments and activities.

colonialism In the modern world, colonialism is defined as the control of one people or nation by another. The military power of the colonizing nation kept the colony under control. Colonialism differs from imperialism in that the colony was claimed to be legally owned by the colonizing nation. Colonialism is not the same as racism. Peoples and nations of all races and in all parts of the world have been colonial powers at one time or another.

fedayeen The Palestinian and Egyptian irregular (nonuniformed) soldiers attacking Israel were called fedayeen. Fedayeen is usually translated as "men of sacrifice." They were irregular paramilitary forces.

imperialism In the modern world, the control of one people or nation by another. The economic and political powers of the imperial nation were usually the most important methods of control. The military power of the imperial nation was used whenever needed to keep the weaker nation under control. The major difference between imperialism and colonialism is that under imperialism a weaker state was not claimed to be the property of the imperialist nation.

irregular forces Irregular forces are not members of a nation's regular military organizations. They can be anything from uncontrolled groups of armed individuals to highly organized scouts, guerrillas, and paramilitary units working with a regular military. Their leaders are outside of regular military chains of command. Their weapons are usually a grab bag of old and new arms. Often, they do not have uniforms.

Zionism A political movement in Europe that started during the last half of the nineteenth century. The main belief was that Jews were a nation without a country and should have a country of their own in Israel/ Palestine. Russian and eastern European violence against Jews was severe in the nineteenth century. Together with anti-Semitism in central and western Europe, this spurred the development of Zionism.

Organizations

Embassy of the Arab Republic of Egypt
3521 International Court NW
Washington, DC 20008
(202) 895 5400
Web site: http://www.embassyofegyptwashingtondc.org

Embassy of Israel
3514 International Drive NW
Washington, DC 20008
(202) 364-5500
Web site: http://www.israelemb.org

Middle East Studies Association of North America
c/o The University of Arizona
1219 N. Santa Rita Avenue
Tucson, AZ 85721
(520) 621-5850
Web site: http://w3fp.arizona.edu/mesassoc

Web Sites

Due to the changing nature of Internet links, the Rosen Publishing Group, Inc., has developed an online list of Web sites related to the subject of this book. This site is updated regularly. Please use this link to access the list:

http://www.rosenlinks.com/wcme/suzr

Adams, Michael. *Suez and After: Year of Crisis*. Boston: Beacon Press, 1958.

Black, Ian, and Benny Morris. *Israel's Secret Wars: A History of Israel's Intelligence Services*. New York: Grove Weidenfeld, 1991.

Dupuy, R. Ernest, and Trevor N. Dupuy. *The Harper Encyclopedia of Military History: From 3500 B.C. to the Present*, 5th edition. New York: HarperCollins, 1993.

Marshall, S. L. A. *Sinai Victory: Command Decisions in History's Shortest War*. New York: William Morrow and Company, 1958.

Schonfield, Hugh J. *The Suez Canal in Peace and War, 1869–1969*. Coral Gables, FL: University of Miami Press, 1968.

BIBLIOGRAPHY

Adams, Michael. *Suez and After: Year of Crisis*. Boston: Beacon Press, 1958.

Black, Ian, and Benny Morris. *Israel's Secret Wars: A History of Israel's Intelligence Services*. New York: Grove Weidenfeld, 1991.

Burnes, Lieutenant General E. L. M. *Between Arab and Israeli*. New York: Ivan Obolensky, 1962.

Dayan, Moshe. *Diary of the Sinai Campaign*. Jerusalem, Israel: Steimatzk's Agency Limited, 1965.

Dupuy, R. Ernest, and Trevor N. Dupuy. *The Harper Encyclopedia of Military History: From 3500 B.C. to the Present*, 5th edition. New York: HarperCollins, 1993.

Fisher, Eugene M., and M. Cherif Bassiouni. *Storm Over the Arab World*. Chicago: Follett Publishing Company, 1972.

Fisher, Sydney Nettleton. *The Middle East: A History*, 2nd Edition. New York: Alfred A. Knopf, 1968.

Georges-Picot, Jacques. Translated from the French by W. G. Roges. *The Real Suez Crisis: The End of a Great Nineteenth Century Work*. New York: Harcourt Brace Jovanovich, 1975.

Marshall, S. L. A. *Sinai Victory: Command Decisions in History's Shortest War*. New York: William Morrow and Company, 1958.

Morris, Benny. *Israel's Border Wars, 1949–1956: Arab Infiltration, Israeli Retaliation, and the Countdown to the Suez War*. Oxford: Clarendon Press, 1993.

Neff, Donald. *Warriors at Suez*. New York: Simon & Schuster, 1981.

Nutting, Anthony. *No End of a Lesson: The Story of Suez*. New York: Carkson N. Potter, 1967.

Pinkus, Binyamin. "Atomic Power to Israel's Rescue: French-Israeli Nuclear Cooperation, 1949–1957." *Israel Studies*, Volume 7, Number 1, pp. 104–138.

Pollack, Kenneth M. *Arabs at War: Military Effectiveness, 1948–1991*. Lincoln, NE: University of Nebraska Press, 2002.

Porch, Douglas. *The French Secret Services*. New York: Farrar, Straus and Giroux, 1995.

Schonfield, Hugh J. *The Suez Canal in Peace and War, 1869–1969*. Coral Gables, FL: University of Miami Press, 1968.

Stock, Ernest. *Israel on the Road to Sinai, 1949–1956*. Ithaca, NY: Cornell University Press, 1967.

INDEX

About the Author

James Fiscus is a Portland, Oregon, writer and photo-journalist. He has a master's degree in Middle East and Asian history and has taught military history. In addition to writing about history, he reports on medicine, science, business, and law.

Photo Credits

Cover © Corbis; pp. 1, 3, 24–25, 28, 46, 48–49, 50 © Hulton/Archive/Getty Images; pp. 4–5 © Hulton-Deutsch Collection/Corbis; pp. 6, 7, 34, 41 © Perry-Castãnedia Library Map Collection/The University of Texas at Austin; pp. 8–9 © Scheufler Collection/Corbis; pp. 12, 20, 54 © AP/Wide World Photos; pp. 16, 18, 22, 32–33, 38, 43, 45, 53 © Bettmann/Corbis; p. 54 © Stringer Oded Balilty/AP/Wide World Photos.

Designer: Nelson Sá; **Editor:** Mark Beyer; **Photo Researcher:** Nelson Sá

SUGAR GROVE PUBLIC LIBRARY DISTRICT
54 Snow Street/P.O. Box 1049
Sugar Grove, IL 60554
(630) 466-4686